Wish You Were Here?

Wish You Were Here?

Poems by Judith Nicholls

Oxford University Press
Oxford New York Toronto

Oxford University Press, Walton Street,
Oxford OX2 6DP

Oxford New York Toronto
Delhi Bombay Calcutta Madras Karachi
Petaling Jaya Singapore Hong Kong Tokyo
Nairobi Dar es Salaam Cape Town
Melbourne Auckland

and associated companies in
Berlin Ibadan

Oxford is a trade mark of Oxford University Press

Illustrated by Bill Piggins

Hardback: ISBN 0 19 276101 3
Paperback: ISBN 0 19 276111 0

A CIP catalogue record for this book is available from
the British Library

Typeset by Pentacor PLC, High Wycombe, Bucks.
Printed in Great Britain

For Gramp,
who knew how to laugh.

1907–1991.

All Aboard!

Hurry, scurry, in the car!
Push that dog down, lock the door!
Where's my bucket? In the boot;
move that deckchair off my foot!

Are we in now? Wait a minute,
here's a shoe with no one in it!
Bats and buckets, spades and balls,
plastic macs for sudden squalls . . .

Hurry, scurry; lock the door!
Get that dog down on the floor!
Hurry, scurry; wait for me!
Who'll be first to see the sea?

Food and chairs and picnic bag,
Grandpa, Sue, the boys, the dog;
Mum with maps and sandwich box,
Dad white-legged in winter socks . . .

Hurry, scurry; lock that door—
this poor car will take no more!
Hurry, scurry; turn the key,
we're off at last to see the sea!

Family Outing

Dad.
His face is set.
Between his fiddling with the keys
(the boot is stuck)
and random orders
(all ignored)
he deals out random gloom.
It's bound to rain,
the clouds are black.
The journey's much too long
for Gramp.
Those chairs won't fit.
If that dog's sick
it's walking back—
I've said a hundred times
THERE ISN'T ROOM!

    Mum
       struggles with the map.
    Her feet are pressed
    between a cricket bat,
    an outsize flask, a fishing reel.
    She's done her bit
    and has a martyred look

but still can't rest.
Her head is full
of sandwiches and swimsuits,
towels, suntan oil,
rubber rings and kites;

of headache pills and sudden chills,
of grazes, drying lips and sunburn,
cream for insect bites.

Susan sulks.
She hates these 'family treats',
would rather stay behind
but Mum said *No!*
Her best friend's back from Spain,
all golden brown
with tales of sea and sun
and Spanish waiters keen to learn
an English word or two.
She secretly agrees with Dad
(*It's bound to rain*)
and keeps her winter face . . .
but packs her hairbrush
and her new bikini,
just in case.

Pete's indifferent.
His mate's away,
he might as well join in,
though doesn't care too much
for weekend jaunts.
He packs a comic,
bat and fishing rod,
and cadges coppers for the fair.

Sam is seven;
sea is heaven,
life is fun.
Quite unaware
of gloomy faces round,
he fills the car
with spades and spoons and laughter;

plans moats and castles by the sea,
and smiles so much that even Dad
can't really quite be cross.
He snuggles close to Grandpa for the ride,
his thoughts already pink
with rock and candyfloss.

Gramp
is in another world.
His trunks, all mothball-fresh,
are pressed against his *Sunday Mail*.

A hankie for his head,
a clutch of dreams
to spread beneath
are all he needs.

Bats and buckets, spades and balls,
plastic macs for sudden squalls;
food and chairs and picnic bag,
sleeping Gramp, impatient dog!

Maps all crumpled, leaking box,
Dad now sweating in his socks . . .
Wake up, Gramp, now: one, two, three!
We're here at last, we're by the SEA!

To the Beach!

Dad, in charge again,
comes to a sudden halt;
surveys the new terrain,
distributes backpacks, ammunition
for the grand assault
(and macs for rain).

Grandpa, wakened by the jolt,
is quite bemused,
whilst Peanuts fills the air
with legs and hair
and frantic tail—
attempts a daring roof escape
(destined to fail),
lands on the company's stores
and gives a sorry wail.

At last they're out.
Adjusting battle-dress
(the famous socks)
Dad marshals all his troops.
Rations for the day
are checked
(as Peanuts licks his lips)

and Sue steps out,
adjusting shorts
on swaying hips
to meet the fray.

Left . . . left . . .
Left, right, left . . .

Bodies spread on rippled sand,
shelters braced against the wind . . .
Here's a gap . . .
No, that's too small,
that will never take us all!
Left . . . left . . .
Left, right, left . . .

There's a good one,
claim that space!
Gather round now,
here's our base!

Platoon—HALT!

To the Sea!

Who'll be first?
Shoes off,
in a row,
four legs fast,
two legs slow—
Ready now?
Off we go!
Tip-toe,
dip-a-toe,
heel and toe—
Yes or no?
Cold as snow!
All at once,
in we go!
One,
    two,
        three,
            SPLASH!

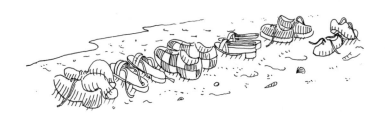

Floating Song

A glimpse of sun
and suddenly—
the world's afloat!

Toddlers gripped in rubber rings,
balding uncles, paleface aunts,
seagulls, poised with folded wings—
all join in the bobbing dance.
Fishing floats and pleasure boats,

pedalos and reed,
flotsam, jetsam,
cups and pails,
driftwood
(left by winter's gales),
lilos, dinghies,
surfboard sails
and streamers of seaweed.

Rise and fall,
rise and fall,
rise and fall,
drift . . .

Grandpa

blossoms
out and up
over the weary waistband
of his trunks
(they must have seen
a hundred years of wear!)
knots his frayed hankie
like a parachute
to cover fraying hair
then eases down.

In less than half an hour
the *Sunday Mail* has slipped,
its rustle masking
Grandpa's gentle snore.
Sun and the journey,
age and the salt-sea air
return him to an earlier trip
(*When I was young . . .*)
The paper crumples,
slides to the sand
beneath his bulging chair.
Softly he sighs for summers lost;
snores loudly into sleep,

then settles dreams and flesh
more deeply in the canvas,
layer by layer.

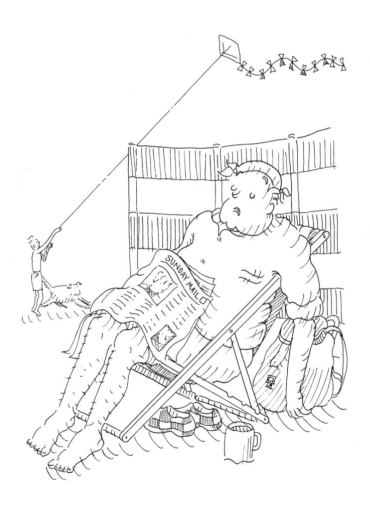

Picnic

George, lend a hand
and spread that cloth,
the sand is everywhere!
Just look at that,
you'd never think
it took hours to prepare!

WAKE UP, GRAMP!
Your food's all out,
get it while you can!
Have a lemonade before
it warms up in the sun.

What is it, Mum?

There's . . .

ham with sand,
and spam with sand,
there's chicken paste
and lamb with sand;
oranges, bananas,
lemonade or tea;
bread with sand

all spread with sand—
at least the sand comes free!
We've crisps with sand
and cake with sand—
it's grand with lunch or tea—
crunch it up,
enjoy it, love,
at least we're by the sea!

Fish Pie with Orchestra

You can scrabble with a scallop
     or a lobster,
you can tussle with a mussel
     or a crab;
you can whet your appetite
     with whelks or winkles,
or dangle from the pier
     for plaice or dab.

You can hear the noisy
     oyster-catcher fishing,
the ringing of the curlew's
     long 'coo-lee';
the tapping of the turnstone
     seeking supper,
the whispered song sung by
     the rolling sea.

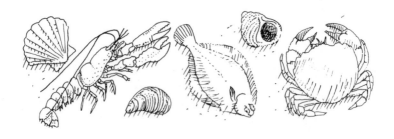

Trumpet Voluntary

The squall has stopped
and on the pier
they start to clear
the waiting stand.
Mum grabs a sulking Susan,
takes the hand of Sam
(his face is lost
in candyfloss),
heads for the dripping seats.
Installed on plastic macs,
still damp and trailing sand
they wait, then hear at last
the sounds of wind through brass:
here comes the band!

The bandsmen, ruddy-faced
(though not from sun)
emerge in disarray.
Conspicuous in royal blue
they shuffle to the stand,
raise trumpets,
Adam's apples
bobbing at their throats.
The crowd is still;
the trumpets fill the air

as, hamster-cheeked,
the bandsmen give their all
(with just a few wrong notes).

Susan drifts;
the trumpets turn to strings,
plucked by dark fingers
on deep-throat wood guitars.
Behind her eyes
the grey skies turn
to Spanish sun . . .
A rose appears
with silk lace fan
and sparkling wine;
its cooling magic
trickles down her throat . . .

Sam rudely nudges,
passes lemonade (in can);
she wakes to hear
the last discordant note.

Sounds of the Fair

Follow the hurdy-gurdy man!

Pete wanders to the fairground,
drawn by sound:
a barrel organ,
carousel,
a skeleton's unnerving wail
(its echo holds him to the ground)—
the fair is *sound*.

Follow the hurdy-gurdy man!

Pete hesitates
and stares around.
The dodgems? Dipper?
Quickly turns his back
against that lurch of car
on downward track;
now hears what sounds
like distant drums
and follows,
half in wonder
half in fear,
to join the crowd.

The drums roll on.
They cheer
then gasp out loud
with one accord
as spangled showman
swallows fire and sword.

Follow the hurdy-gurdy man!

Now one last time
Pete turns his back,
heads for a different sound,
the crack of pellets
on the rifle range;
feels for his change
then, fingers trembling,
loads the barrel,
lifts his rifle high.
A bull's-eye first time round?
He'll surely try!

Drama on the Pier!

Dad, mesmerized
by dreams of mighty fish,
stares at his bobbing float.
No twitch of rod or reel
until, at last,
some floundering victim
large as any dream
drifts into sight.
Grasp tightens,
expectations rise;
just seconds now
before the bait is found.
A token fight
and then . . .
to land the longed-for prize!

But wait . . .

Below, bedraggled,
drowning in wet hair and foam,
bemused by each succeeding wave . . .
THAT WRETCHED DOG!
I KNEW HE SHOULD HAVE STAYED AT HOME!
Is Dad's face red . . .
but what to do?
Where's Mum? Where's Pete?
Or Gramp or Sam or Sue?
The fishermen stay put,
though plenty stare.
He spies a ladder
lurching out of sight
towards the tide
(quite vertical, prohibited
except in case of fire);
discreetly trying to hide
his burning face
he clambers down—
before a growing crowd.

HEY, YOU!
GET BACK,
THAT'S NOT ALLOWED!

The lifeguard's angry shouts
bring Mum and Sue
(and many more)
to see just who
has dared defy this man,
the undefiable,
this voice of seaside law.
Too late.
Dad, fully-clothed and shod
now splutters through the waves
towards the wretched dog.
The grateful creature wriggles wildly,
tries to lick his thanks . . .
but Dad is breathless now
and weak with cold.
His knees are stiff,
the current strong.
Weighed down by trousers, sweater,
jacket, shoes and dog,
he can't hold out for long
and struggles, half-submerged
to grab the nearby sign:
BATHING PROHIBITED.
Next time, he swears,

that dog stays on its lead—
or else the wretched creature
learns to read.

Help is at hand!
To noisy cheers,
the lifeguard
(twenty-two and muscles
rippled as the sand)
strips off
before the gasping crowd;
dives from the pier.

Sue, now wide awake,
with breath more baited
than her father's rod,
sees only hairy-chested bronze,
is dazzled by the ease
with which he tows the pair
through rising seas;
flicks fingers through her much-combed hair,
sees them head towards the beach,
hurries to meet them there . . .

Winter Gardens

Hair rinsed and neatly pressed
in forties curls,
patent shoes and stocking seams;
skirts flowered and full
for dainty twirls
and steps from dancing lessons
fixed in dreams . . .

One two three,
One two three,
Just let it flow;
Keep those feet
Moving and
Smile as you go!
Arm round your
Partner, space
Out on the
Floor; now it's
One two three,
Waltz with me,
Try that once more!

One two three,
One two three,
Play for us now;
Tunes that we
Danced to a
Long time ago!
One two three
Now, while the
Organist
Plays, let me
Waltz with you
Here till the
End of our days!

(The two choruses are to be performed
simultaneously).

Rocking the Boat!

Go for it, man!

The dream is halted
by a rev of bikes
and sudden entrance of a motley crowd
whose colours rival any lights.
Not only blue, but green and red,
with orange, lilac, purple-tips,
quite rigid on the leader's head.
Fine in leather, metal studs,
in safety-pins and shoulder-pads,
they come with denim-coated girls
and quite outshine the forties curls.

The management are paralysed—
for several seconds stand like stone
(each wishing he had stayed at home).
The waltzers all retreat in pairs
as from our leader's bristly neck
a loud transistor wildly flares . . .

Soon realization dawns.
Not THIS place, man—
the OTHER one!
Before the management awakes—
a noisy exit, screech of brakes.
Illegal revving,
throttle groans,
a few loud curses,
further moans—
then all is quiet.
The waltz resumes.

Lord Neptune

Build me a castle,
the young boy cried,
as he tapped his father's knee.
But make it tall
and make it wide,
with a king's throne just for me.

An echo drifted on the wind,
sang deep and wild and free:
Oh you can be king of the castle,
but I am lord of the sea.

Give me your spade,
the father cried;
let's see what we can do!
We'll make it wide
so it holds the tide,
with a fine throne just for you.

He dug deep down
in the firm damp sand,
for the tide was falling fast.
The moat was deep,

the ramparts high,
and the turrets tall and vast.

Now I am king,
the young boy cried,
and this is my golden throne!
I rule the sands,
I rule the seas;
I'm lord of all lands, alone!

The sand-king ruled
from his golden court
and it seemed the wind had died;
but at dusk his throne
sank gently down
in Neptune's rolling tide.

And an echo rose upon the wind,
sang deep and wild and free:
Oh you may be king of the castle,
but I am lord of the sea.

Dusk

The beach has cleared.
All but a stalwart few
(young sweethearts,
tramps or local dogs)
have emptied shoes
of stones and sand,
retreated to the prom.
With hands and spirit warmed
by local fish and chips,
each one reviews his day.

The sun is low across the bay,
changes the shape of things,
casts magic over what was not.
The beach-day's litter
fades into a kindly gloom;
the clock-tower, dull at noon,
now turns to magic Camelot
and visions of enchanted nights
are stirred as, one by one,
a thousand wandering stars
give way to endless lights.

Time for Home!

Grandpa yawns, eyes almost shut.
Four legs settle on his foot;
dry at last and full of food
just for once the dog's subdued.

Pete dreams of bull's-eyes,
beating marksmen twice his size;
Sam, with pockets full of sand,
clutches shells in sticky hand.

Move along, there's one more chair;
it will never fit in there!
Move along—how time has flown!
All aboard, it's time for home.

Mum still hums a dancing tune,
Sue's forgotten Spain in June;
treasures one small secret glance,
dreams of rescues—and romance.

Dad, clothes wet and lips still white,
wears Sue's sweater (much too tight),
fiddles now with keys and locks,
sheepish in pink mac and socks.

Move along now, lock that door!
Grandpa's number one to snore.
Minutes later, not a peep;
all but Dad are sound asleep.